Selected Haiku

Nicholas A. Virgilio

Selected Haiku

Second Edition, Augmented

Introduction by Rod Willmot

Burnt Lake Press

Black Moss Press

Front cover photo by J. Kyle Keener,
reprinted with permission from
The Philadelphia Inquirer, May 27, 1987.

Dépôt légal – 3e trimestre 1988
Bibliothéque nationale du Québec

Second Edition co-published by
Burnt Lake Press, 535 Duvernay, Sherbrooke,
P.Q., Canada J1L 1Y8
and
Black Moss Press, P.O. Box 143, Station A,
Windsor, Ontario, Canada N9A 6L7

Black Moss books are distributed in
Canada and the United States by
Firefly Books, Ltd., 3520 Pharmacy Avenue, Unit 1C,
Scarborough, Ontario, Canada M1W 2T8.

Typeset in Joanna and printed in Canada by
The Coach House Press (Toronto).

Canadian Cataloguing in Publication Data

Virgilio, Nicholas A. (Nicholas Anthony), 1928-
    Selected Haiku

2nd ed. augm.
ISBN 0-920349-05-6 (Burnt Lake Press) –
ISBN 0-88753-180-6 (Black Moss Press)

1. Haiku, American.   I. Title.

PS3572.I73S44 1988   811'.54   C88-090224-8

For my parents and patrons, Anthony and Rose Virgilio,
and for my brothers, Larry and Tony

Introduction

The first edition of this book was printed on a table-top letter-press and painstakingly bound by hand. Miraculously, it was chosen for review on National Public Radio, where Nick Virgilio later became a frequent commentator. Weeks after those first few minutes of airtime, I began to receive orders from listeners all over the United States, individuals who had gone to great lengths to find the address of an obscure Canadian publisher. It was then that I realized the strength of Virgilio's popular appeal. He is a poet who overstrides the restrictions of time and space and literary convention, a poet who speaks to readers from all levels of society, even if they have never before heard of haiku. Yet at the same time he is a respected figure in the sometimes rarefied circles of haiku specialists.

Virgilio's first appearance in a haiku magazine was in 1963, with a single haiku published in the inaugural issue of *American Haiku*:

> Spring wind frees
> the full moon tangled
> in leafless trees.

In its use of rhyme, this poem reflects the strongest literary influence on Virgilio's writing: the translations of Japanese haiku in H.G. Henderson's *An Introduction to Haiku*. Although the Japanese do not use rhyme, Henderson believed that English-language poets would need it to help recreate the formal unity of Japanese haiku. He was wrong, however, for in the vast body of haiku written in English over the last 20 years, rhyme is extremely rare. Only Virgilio has gone on to use it with any frequency.

But there is something else to notice about the haiku above: it is an illusion. Early haiku often have an illusional quality about them; traces of it can even be found in two much better haiku (here in their original form) for which Virgilio became famous:

> Lily:
> out of the water ...
> out of itself.

> Bass
>> picking bugs
>> off the moon!

The first of these has been widely imitated, while the second is credited by another fine poet, John Wills, with starting him on the path of his own development in haiku. Both poems contributed dramatically to liberating haiku poets from the 5-7-5 tradition of syllabic versification. Yet in the content of each there is something that does not quite accord with reality: perhaps not an unreality, but an attempt to lay bare a different kind of reality.

Partly out of a need for relief from North America's materialistic positivism, many haiku poets in the 60's adopted the new vision of reality offered in the Zen-inspired writings of R.H. Blyth, such as his book *Zen in English Literature and Oriental Classics*. In haiku, the Zen influence translated into an intense focus upon the 'suchness' of things, reality as it could only be discovered in moments of acute perception. As poets were thus sharpening their senses and paring down their haiku, illusions evaporated. But already Nick Virgilio was turning in yet another direction, toward reality as it is known by ordinary men and women in their daily lives. No doubt this was his natural inclination; but if one decisive event was needed to plunge his writing irrevocably into the fullness of life, it was the death of his younger brother in Viet Nam. Here was a grimness that could not be prettified, a turmoil that could not be stilled. Later there would also be reconciliation, hope, and laughter. But from this point on Virgilio could no longer transport his reader to a lily as if the world had ceased to turn. You read him now with your feet on the ground, your heart beating.

Among the many themes in Virgilio's haiku there are a few that return obsessively, as if refusing to leave him in peace:

> always returning
> to the terminal patient's toe –
> autumn fly

But often I think it is the toe that returns to the fly, as the prophet wrestles with the angel and will not let go. This is a poet who refuses to be satisfied with the first answer to anything. For there are things in life that are so complex, so mysterious in their mixture of rightness and pain, that to speak of them only once would be to let them off lightly, and learn nothing. As a result of Virgilio's stubborn grip on life, he is rooted in a world that is deep in all directions. Things, people, events, all are replete with meaning, with emotional echoes, as in this remembrance of his brother's death:

> sixteenth autumn since:
> the barely visible grease marks
> where he parked his car

Sometimes the echo in Virgilio's haiku has a spiritual note. With a technique that is at once related and opposed to the illusions of the early haiku, he will say something false in order to imply something true. Or he will say something unremarkably factual in order to imply something extraordinary, something that if stated outright would not be believed.

> the cathedral bell
> is shaking a few snowflakes
> from the morning air

> autumn twilight:
> the wreath on the door
> lifts in the wind

I mentioned technique. A few years ago a journalist who had been overly impressed by Nick's unrestrained personality called me to ask, 'But can the guy write?' 'He certainly can,' I answered. In haiku, the best technique is usually invisible, and what looks easy as pie has been cooked with consummate skill. But here is an example where any reader can appreciate the poet's ability:

> approaching autumn:
> the warehouse watchdog's bark
> weakens in the wind

It is as if the dog's woof were being reduced to w. We actually hear it ... w— w— w— w ... and there is something weak and whining about the creature, like the fly, like the devil who nags us from within with his endless nay-saying. Compare that with a more recent haiku:

9

barking its breath
into the rat-hole:
bitter cold

Instead of *w* we hear *b*, forthright and powerful. The villain is no longer the dog but an unseen rat. Everything has changed. Partly because the word 'dog' is cleverly left out, we can see in this animal a reflection of ourselves: our own tenacious vigour in an often harsh world.

The front cover of this book will call to mind another example of tenacious vigour: the poet Walt Whitman. Virgilio was a prime mover in the founding of The Walt Whitman Center for the Arts and Humanities, in Camden, New Jersey. In Nick Virgilio's poems I hear the same 'barbaric yawp' that Whitman sounded over the rooftops of the world. Is it too audacious to suggest that if Whitman were writing now, given the state of America and her literature today, he just might be a haiku poet?

Some final notes about the text. In selecting and arranging the haiku for this edition I have tried to let them tell their own story, placing together those that speak best in each other's company. The order is loosely biographical, not chronological. Since Virgilio's presentation has grown simpler over the years, and over a third of the haiku were written after the first edition was published, I have rendered them all in the uncluttered style he now prefers.

Virgilio is a prolific writer, and only a fraction of his haiku output appears in these pages. To borrow an analogy from baseball – fitting for so American a poet – he is the kind of batter who frequently strikes out, yet whose mighty swing, whenever it connects, produces an effect far greater than the timid efforts of more consistent players. In all of the haiku here, Virgilio connects solidly. Most readers will agree that this is a poet who knows how to hit home, and does so time and again.

Rod Willmot

heat before the storm:
a fly disturbs the quiet
of the empty store

the knifegrinder's bell
fades in the afternoon heat:
cicada

always returning
to the turd on the tombstone:
cemetery flies

a tiny butterfly
is helping little brother
forget the heat

the empty highway:
a tiger swallowtail
follows the divider

incoming fog
is covering rocks and rusty hulls
with flocks of gulls

a distant balloon
drifting over the county fair
eclipses the moon

the retarded boy asks
'Do you own that?'
The muddy creek

lake lilies open:
a white heron turns its head
towards the sun

the deranged boy
stops babbling:
cicada

deep in rank grass,
through a bullet-riddled helmet:
an unknown flower

In memory of Lawrence J. Virgilio

telegram in hand,
the shadow of the marine
darkens our screen door

the autumn wind
has torn the telegram and more
from mother's hand

into the blinding sun ...
the funeral procession's
glaring headlights

removing the shroud:
mother and father alone
step out of the crowd

beneath the coffin
at the edge of the open grave:
the crushed young grass

flag-covered coffin:
the shadow of the bugler
slips into the grave

my gold star mother
and father hold each other
and the folded flag

Thanksgiving dinner:
placing the baby's high chair
in the empty space

on the darkened wall
of my dead brother's bedroom:
the dates and how tall

the first snowfall:
down the cellar staircase
my father calls

bitter cold wind
carving a frozen snowdrift:
the crescent moon

my dead brother ...
wearing his gloves and boots
I step into deep snow

the sack of kittens
sinking in the icy creek
increases the cold

the cathedral bell
is shaking a few snowflakes
from the morning air

rising and falling ...
a blanket of blackbirds feeds
on the snowy slope

the bare maple sways,
and a tire on a wire cable
swings in the spring air

Easter morning ...
the sermon is taking the shape
of her neighbor's hat

lone red-winged blackbird
riding a reed in high tide –
billowing clouds

over spatterdocks,
turning at corners of air:
dragonfly

lily:
out of the water ...
out of itself

bass
picking bugs
off the moon

now the days are long
through the blazing heat and haze:
sprays of sparrow song

empty farmhouse:
moon in the rain barrel
hatching mosqitoes

one wild apple
ripples the rain puddle:
evening sun

the town clock's face
adds another shade of yellow
to the afterglow

town barberpole
stops turning:
autumn nightfall

now the swing is still:
a suspended tire
centers the autumn moon

shaking the muskrat –
snow falls from the trapper's hair –
and from a reed

a crow in the snowy pine ...
inching up a branch,
letting the evening sun through

winter evening:
leaving father's footprints
I sink into deep snow

down from the stone bridge,
alone in the darkness:
the star in the creek

on the bedroom floor,
tying the umbilical cord:
March snowstorm

For my father

pinned to the altar,
lifting in the autumn wind:
pictures of the dead

adding father's name
to the family tombstone
with room for my own

alone on the road
in the wake of the hearse
dust on my shoes

at the open grave,
mingling with the priest's prayer:
honking of wild geese

after father's wake,
the long walk in the moonlight
to the darkened house

the fork in the road:
a fallen fingerpost
points to the autumn moon

the graduation ring
slips from my finger:
the midnight river

the long winding road:
a run-over rattlesnake
writhing in the sun

autumn twilight:
the wreath on the door
lifts in the wind

after the bell,
within the silence:
within myself

Thanksgiving alone:
ordering eggs and toast
in an undertone

taking a hard look
at myself from all angles –
the men's store mirrors

the cold ashes of the Phoenix
in the empty box of Kleenex

not a breath of air
in the crowded cathedral:
the sermon on Hell

cathedral silence:
deaf mute penitents enter
the confessional

the funeral Mass:
in the holy water fount
confetti and rice

having come this far
alive at fifty-five:
the morning star

running my finger
along the crack in the bell:
this Independence Day

where cattle graze
near the grassy battleground:
the grave mounds of slaves

the flag's shadow
creeps toward the crater:
footprints on the moon

January launch:
in the space shuttle's shadow
astronauts gather

the far graveyard
quivering in the heat wave:
river at my feet

the junkyard dog
in the shadow of the shack:
the heat

boarding the wrong bus: the heat

her shadow shaving the hair from its legs: the heat

removing
the bullet-proof vest:
the heat

raising their voices
discussing Reaganomics:
hookers on the bus

between tricks knitting booties

shadowing hookers
after dark:
the cross in the park

in the empty church
at nightfall, a lone firefly
deepens the silence

approaching autumn:
the warehouse watchdog's bark
weakens in the wind

slipping past the guard
and over the barbed wire fence:
wind-blown newspaper

autumn tornado
buckles the billboard:
her torn smile

stirring the soup with my finger: night of love

the scent of semen penetrates her loneliness

Litany for the Dead

at the slave auction,
missing from the ship's manifest:
the names of the dead

on the Wailing Wall
unveiled by the autumn wind:
the names of the dead

on the newspaper
blown against the barbed wire fence:
the names of the dead

the patrol report
unfolding in the cold wind:
the names of the dead

on the petition
condemning Agent Orange:
the names of the dead

read aloud
to the head of Union Carbide:
the names of the dead

St. Valentine's Day:
pinned to the police report
the names of the dead

on time cards
at the entrance to the mine:
the names of the dead

gladiola bulbs
wrapped in old newspaper:
the names of the dead

November morning:
dropping the names of the dead
in the ballot box

the first snowfall
is coating a small stack
of rusty cannon balls

the blind musician
extending an old tin cup
collects a snowflake

the icy river:
a drowned wino washed ashore
eyes the morning moon

on the frozen snow
etched with tire tracks and fire hose:
the stretcher's shadow

barking its breath
into the rat-hole:
bitter cold

New Year's Eve:
pay phone receiver
dangling

empty ballroom ...
basking in the moonlight:
fallen mask

in the singles' bar
magnifying loneliness:
her thick eye glasses

on the cardboard box
holding the frozen wino:
Fragile: Do Not Crush

For Father Michael Doyle

exploring the wild
on public television –
the latch-key child

my palsied mother,
pressing my forehead on hers
this Ash Wednesday

cold morning rain –
gathering under the canopy,
friends of the mobster

chasing a fly
from the communion bread:
the Mass for the Dead

ringing the church bell
for the Farm Workers' Mass:
the rope burn

beyond empty pews
darkened to a dying candle:
a bell tolls and tolls

from the willow
it fell into the empty grave:
cicada shell

my dead brother ...
hearing his laugh
in my laughter

atop the town flagpole,
a gob of bubblegum
holds my dead brother's dime

sixteenth autumn since:
barely visible grease marks
where he parked his car

the old neighborhood
falling to the wrecking ball:
names in the sidewalk

the old neighborhood
with fresh paint and new faces:
the whores up the street

morning sun:
my shadow walking
swinging its arms

my spring love affair:
the old upright Remington
wears a new ribbon

rolled and folded
it fits the hole in the screen:
green rejection slip

my palsied mother
forcing her hands to be still:
staring children

beyond the park bench
carved with hearts and initials:
the war monument

Viet Nam monument
darkened by the autumn rain:
my dead brother's name

where the battlefield
narrows to a cattle path:
the dew on the grass

always returning
to the terminal patient's toe –
autumn fly

starting the New Year
in the ransacked apartment:
heart attack

headlights stare at headlights: foggy crossroads

spentagon
pentagony
repentagon

so many names on the monument reflecting passersby

Hiroshimagined

nowl

blossomnipresence

marshawkwardove

stillocustill

her photograph fades:
the widower at the window
shadows the torn shade

newspaper shading my eyes: honking of wild geese

another autumn:
still silent in his closet
father's violin

the grove by the creek:
crows echoing each other
reach out in the mist

hospital quiet
I enter alone at twilight:
the scent of lilacs

For Richard Wilbur

palsied hands touching
the dusty sewing machine:
sunlight through the blinds

on my last journey
alone on the road at dawn:
first sight of the sea

The Author

After serving with the U.S. Navy in World War II, Nick Virgilio worked as a radio announcer for many years, and then as a publicist, before retiring to care for his invalid mother. In 1971 he co-directed the First International Haiku Festival, in Philadelphia. He helped establish The Walt Whitman Center for the Arts and Humanities, in Camden, New Jersey, and was its poet-in-residence for 5 years. His haiku, widely published in North America and Japan, much anthologized, and often heard over the electronic media, have received numerous prizes. He has been much involved in giving poetry workshops, lectures and readings, and has been the subject of studies and profiles in places as diverse as the haiku magazines, major daily newspapers, and *Writer's Yearbook*.

Acknowledgements: Many of these poems first appeared in the following magazines: *American Haiku, Asphodel, Brussels Sprout, Cicada, Frogpond, Haiku West, Modern Haiku, Wind Chimes.*